For YOU - 4 Books in 1

How to Discover the Motives of your Behaviour
and the Secrets of Your Subconscious Mind

How to preserve your psychological health

How to Draw your Children

A Workbook

First 100 Sentences

(From Your Creativity)

(A Workbook)

By
Mahmoud

CONTENTS

(1)
How to Discover the Motives of your Behaviour and the Secrets of Your Subconscious Mind

Introduction

How can you discover how prepared you are for a life of improved psychological health, or how ready you are for a state of unrest, psychological turmoil, and instability in your everyday life?

Why do you become angry at someone without knowing the reason?

Why are you fearful of something, someone, or some event, confrontation, or entity without having a clear explanation?

Why do you feel anxious or nervous in certain situations without understanding the cause?

Why do you love one person and hate another, and why is it that when you confront yourself about it, you find no answer?

What are your greatest strengths and weaknesses?

In this book, you will discover the secrets behind the motives of your behaviour, and it will reveal the memories stored in your subconscious mind from the time you were a child until now.

In order to find the answers to all of your questions, simply follow these instructions, then send your feedback to the author:

info@ihossa.com

or

malmostshar@yahoo.com

If you wish to receive the file in Word format, please send us an email message and we will send it to you immediately.

After completing the application, you will receive the full analysis and a report containing the memories of your subconscious mind, and the secrets behind the motives of your behaviour.

Read each word carefully and individually, then record (either in writing or voice) the first thought that comes to your mind when you read the word. There are no right and wrong thoughts, neither are there any ethical nor unethical ones. The accuracy of the results depend on what exactly comes to your mind.

Word	Thought
Woman	

Milk		
Man		
Sun		
Moon		

Tree	
Deprivation	
Chicken	
Car	

Staircase	
Food	
Maid	

Boy

Girl

Country	
Fingers	

House

Ball

Eye	
Game	

Stomach	
Television	

Yesterday

Bride

School

Night

Cartoon

Bed

Room	
Street	

Dog	
Bicycle	

Cat

Mirror

Prayer	
Love	

Childhood	
Adolescence	

Sex	
Water	

Horse	
Me	

Mouth	
Success	

Failure	
Ice	

Tears	
Hand	

Forest	
Heart	

Obesity	
Slenderness	

	Mother
Wall	

Paper	
Fear	

Sorrow

Anger

Father	
Sister	

Brother	
Neighbours	

Adolescence	
Family	

Punishment	
Reward	

Smile	
Picture	

Beauty	
Unconscious	

urination	
Murder	
Blood	

Plane	
Car	

Red light	
Molesting	

Intimacy	
Assault	

Friend	
Girlfriend	

Pleasure
Bird

Freedom

Affection	
Stubbornness	

Pen	
Internet	

Teacher	
Female	

teacher	
Possible	
Peak	

Kitchen	
Party	

Yellow

Red	
Black	

Green	
White	

Blue	
Tree	

Death	
Illness	

Anxiety	
Depression	

Door

Poverty

Wealth	
Darkness	

Sleep	
Day	

Week

Month

Year	
Rose	

Box	
Examination	

Study

How to preserve your psychological health

"How to preserve your psychological health without being influenced by the negative attitudes of others"

In this exercise you will learn how to:

Feel calmer

Relax before and during stressful situations

Face negative thoughts and replace them with positive ones.

CONTENTS

(1)

The psychological equation is:

Your ideas, thoughts, and beliefs influence your behavioural actions and bodily responses.

If your thoughts are negative, your behavioural actions and bodily responses will be negative;

Whereas if your thoughts are positive, your behavioural actions and bodily responses will be positive.

(2)

Look at the photos.

Here we will show you a few photos.

Notice your feelings, whatever they may be. Record them along with your ideas (Choose the method of recording – notes, video, or audio).

(3)

<u>What is required to be done is:</u>

Implement the following steps as part of the training:

1. Relax and breathe deeply, then exhale slowly (3 times).
2. Look at the photo and the negative expressions it bears.
3. Replace those expressions with positive ones (replace sad expressions with happy ones, depression with joy, anger with serenity, and such) while repeating in your mind "I am calm and relaxed; my mind is calm, and I feel inner tranquillity", while smiling.
4. Repeat this with each photo.
5. Overcome any various thoughts that deter you from performing this exercise.
6. After mastering this technique, document your positive state, along with the feelings and ideas that accompany you in this positive state (documenting may be by writing, taking a video of one's self, or taking a personal photo).
7. Send your documented positive state to the trainer for evaluation.

By being able to imagine yourself in your positive state and document it while repeating positive statements while smiling followed by the trainer's evaluation, you will attain the life that you deserve to live.

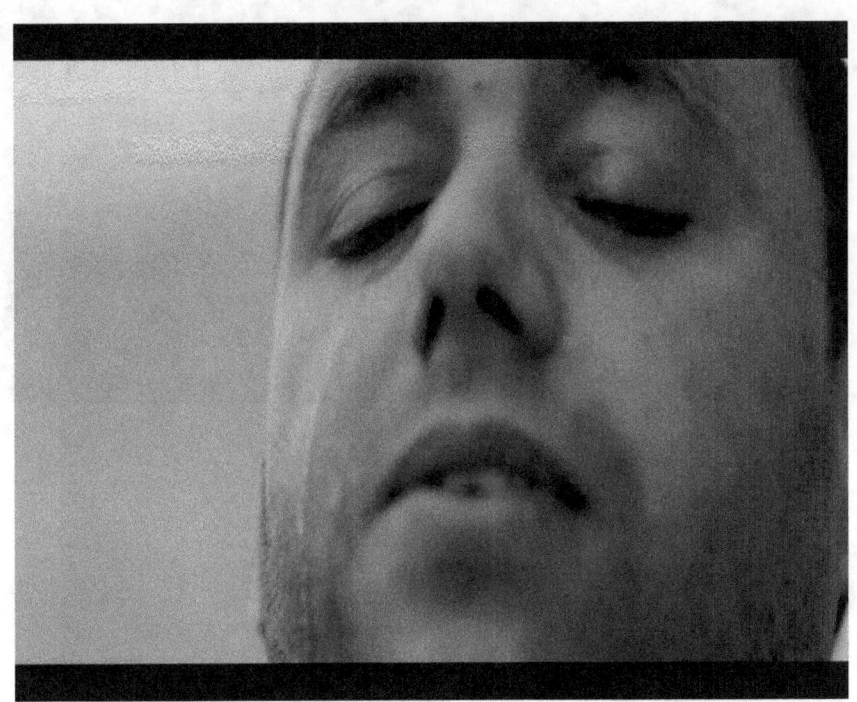

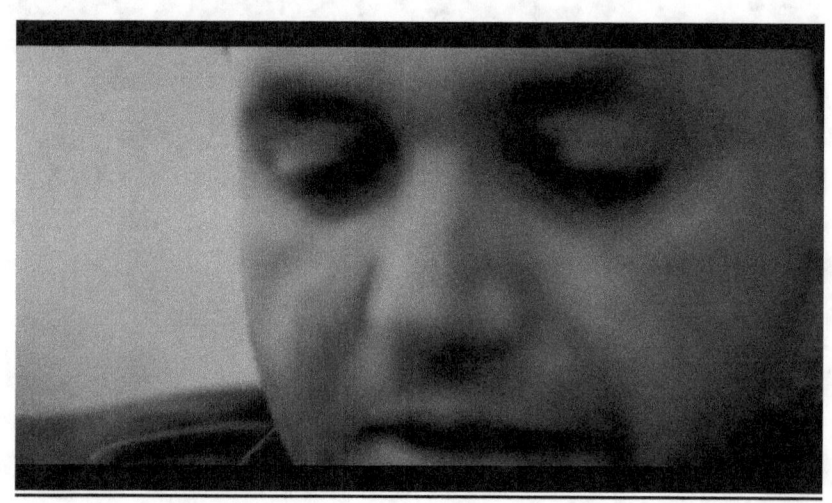

Implement the following steps as part of the training:

1. Relax and breathe deeply, then exhale slowly (3 times).
2. Look at the photo and the negative expressions it bears.
3. Replace those expressions with positive ones (replace sad expressions with happy ones, depression with joy, anger with serenity, and such) while repeating in your mind "I am calm and relaxed; my mind is calm, and I feel inner tranquillity", while smiling.
4. Repeat this with each photo.
5. Overcome any various thoughts that deter you from performing this exercise.
6. After mastering this technique, document your positive state, along with the feelings and ideas that accompany you in this positive state (documenting may be by writing, taking a video of one's self, or taking a personal photo).
7. Send your documented positive state to the trainer for evaluation.

By being able to imagine yourself in your positive state and document it while repeating positive statements while smiling followed by the trainer's evaluation, you will attain the life that you deserve to live.

(3)

How to Draw your Children

A Workbook

Based on his experience as a psychologist and counsellor, the Author poses the question to mothers and fathers; 'how to sculpture your son or daughter' to help them discover the psychological, cognitive, behavioural, physical, and social needs of their children, and to draw out a plan to fulfil those needs and achieve their pedagogical objectives.

This book consists of 28 drawings, and each drawing carries a comment written by the artist (i.e. the mother or father) representing their son's or daughter's needs from the perspective of the parents.

We recommend following the steps below to attain the maximum benefit from this book:

1. Look at the drawing.
2. Read the related comment.
3. Place a tick on the drawing if it applies to your son or daughter, while also placing a tick on the need written next to the drawing if you consider it relevant to your son or daughter.
4. Draw your child by yourself, determine his or her need next to the drawing, then analyse the reasons and specify the following practical steps to fulfil these needs (there should be a separate drawing for each child).

You may contact the author through these email addresses malmostshar@yahoo.com or info@ihossa.com to obtain necessary advice and instructions.

The need for Self-<u>Estimate</u>

The need for Discovering skills and capabilities

The need for Joy and play

The need for Understanding

The need for Support

The need for Self-expression

The need for Independence

The need for Miming and imitating

The need for emotional fulfilment

The need for Listening

The need for Assistance in forming a philosophy for life

The need for Feeling secure

The need for Advice, guidance, and mentoring

The need for Bravery

The need for Dialogue

The need for Comprehension

The need for Incentive and encouragement

The need for Organising time and time management

The need for Achievement

The need for Discovery

The need for Experimentation

The need for Friendship

The need for Self-actualization

The need for Practice on decision-making

The need for Love

The need for Security

The need for Belonging

The need for Healthy food

How to Draw your Children

You may contact the author through these email addresses malmostshar@yahoo.com or info@ihossa.com to obtain necessary advice and instructions.

MAHMOUD

(4)

First 100 Sentences

(From Your Creativity)

(A Workbook)

This book will help both adults and children to:

1. Learn any language using the **Flow** state technique. (The examples in the book are applied to the English language.)
2. Gain fast intuition.
3. Attain unlimited vocabulary.
4. Speak fluently.

The tool:

Flow state is a condition of psychological, behavioural, and cognitive integration and preoccupation with the sought objective (i.e. learning a language) by using elements of the environment in which one lives.

Conditions of applying the flow state technique are:

- Happiness, joy, and love prior, during, and after practical application.
- Psychological and mental concentration and focus.
- Mastering both performance and practice.
- Enthusiasm and self-motivation.
- Evaluation of performance and positive change.

How?

1. One word a day is sufficient (as in the table) in the same manner clarified in the practical example (later).
2. Write what is required as indicated in the table.
3. Effortlessly speak what you write (with yourself, while repeating it, repeating in your mind, then start using it with others).

Example

Word	Table
What	- A piece of furniture with a flat top
Why	- For eating
How	- Best Deals For Your Home · Cash On Delivery (1-5 tables available now)
Picture	

Word	Chair
What	
Why	
How	
Picture	

Word	Glass
What	
Why	
How	
Picture	

Word	Wall
What	
Why	
How	
Picture	

Word	Veranda
What	
Why	
How	
Picture	

Word	Mobile
What	
Why	
How	
Picture	

Word	Electric
What	
Why	
How	
Picture	

Word	Light
What	
Why	
How	
Picture	

Word	Window
What	
Why	
How	
Picture	

Word	Door
What	
Why	
How	
Picture	

Word	Room
What	
Why	
How	
Picture	

Word	Bed
What	
Why	
How	
Picture	

Word	Restroom
What	
Why	
How	
Picture	

Word	Kitchen
What	
Why	
How	
Picture	

Word	Television
What	
Why	
How	
Picture	

Word	Laptop
What	
Why	
How	
Picture	

Word	Sofa
What	
Why	
How	
Picture	

Word	Cable
What	
Why	
How	
Picture	

Word	Soap
What	
Why	
How	
Picture	

Word	Shower
What	
Why	
How	
Picture	

Word	Hair
What	
Why	
How	
Picture	

Word	Land
What	
Why	
How	
Picture	

Word	Wake up
What	
Why	
How	
Picture	

Word	Sleep
What	
Why	
How	
Picture	

Word	Talk
What	
Why	
How	
Picture	

Word	Wife
What	
Why	
How	
Picture	

Word	Husband
What	
Why	
How	
Picture	

Word	Son
What	
Why	
How	
Picture	

Word	Each Morning
What	
Why	
How	
Picture	

Word	Ask
What	
Why	
How	
Picture	

Word	Time
What	
Why	
How	
Picture	

Word	Think
What	
Why	
How	
Picture	

Word	Rest
What	
Why	
How	
Picture	

Word	Wash
What	
Why	
How	
Picture	

Word	Eat
What	
Why	
How	
Picture	

Word	Piece
What	
Why	
How	
Picture	

Word	Fruit
What	
Why	
How	
Picture	

Word	Letter
What	
Why	
How	
Picture	

Word	Yellow
What	
Why	
How	
Picture	

Word	Hungry
What	
Why	
How	
Picture	

Word	Favourite
What	
Why	
How	
Picture	

Word	Happy
What	
Why	
How	
Picture	

Word	Sad
What	
Why	
How	
Picture	

Word	House
What	
Why	
How	
Picture	

Word	Story
What	
Why	
How	
Picture	

Word	Strong
What	
Why	
How	
Picture	

Word	Place
What	
Why	
How	
Picture	

Word	Action
What	
Why	
How	
Picture	

Word	Speaker
What	
Why	
How	
Picture	

Word	Get brushing
What	
Why	
How	
Picture	

Word	See
What	
Why	
How	
Picture	

Word	Hear
What	
Why	
How	
Picture	

Word	Red
What	
Why	
How	
Picture	

Word	Taste
What	
Why	
How	
Picture	

Word	Touch
What	
Why	
How	
Picture	

Word	Smell
What	
Why	
How	
Picture	

Word	Quiet
What	
Why	
How	
Picture	

Word	Salty
What	
Why	
How	
Picture	

Word	Soft
What	
Why	
How	
Picture	

Word	Family
What	
Why	
How	
Picture	

Word	Birthday
What	
Why	
How	
Picture	

Word	Address
What	
Why	
How	
Picture	

Word	Able
What	
Why	
How	
Picture	

Word	Day
What	
Why	
How	
Picture	

Word	Clothing
What	
Why	
How	
Picture	

Word	Building
What	
Why	
How	
Picture	

Word	Paper
What	
Why	
How	
Picture	

Word	Foot
What	
Why	
How	
Picture	

Word	Try
What	
Why	
How	
Picture	

Word	Pray
What	
Why	
How	
Picture	

Word	Say
What	
Why	
How	
Picture	

Word	Keep
What	
Why	
How	
Picture	

Word	Forgive
What	
Why	
How	
Picture	

Word	Work
What	
Why	
How	
Picture	

Word	Back up
What	
Why	
How	
Picture	

Word	Leave
What	
Why	
How	
Picture	

Word	Arrive
What	
Why	
How	
Picture	

Word	Move
What	
Why	
How	
Picture	

Word	Support
What	
Why	
How	
Picture	

Word	Carry on
What	
Why	
How	
Picture	

Word	Relax
What	
Why	
How	
Picture	

Word	Discuss
What	
Why	
How	
Picture	

Word	Watch
What	
Why	
How	
Picture	

Word	Movie
What	
Why	
How	
Picture	

Word	Study
What	
Why	
How	
Picture	

Word	Draw
What	
Why	
How	
Picture	

Word	Mother
What	
Why	
How	
Picture	

Word	Father
What	
Why	
How	
Picture	

Word	Brother
What	
Why	
How	
Picture	

Word	Daughter
What	
Why	
How	
Picture	

Word	Come
What	
Why	
How	
Picture	

Word	Go to
What	
Why	
How	
Picture	

Word	Cooking food
What	
Why	
How	
Picture	

Word	Voice
What	
Why	
How	
Picture	

Word	Face
What	
Why	
How	
Picture	

Word	Doctor
What	
Why	
How	
Picture	

Word	Engineer
What	
Why	
How	
Picture	

Word	Teacher
What	
Why	
How	
Picture	

Word	Coach
What	
Why	
How	
Picture	

Word	Sister
What	
Why	
How	
Picture	

Word	Open
What	
Why	
How	
Picture	

In order to find the answers to all of your questions, simply follow these instructions, then send your feedback to the author:

info@ihossa.com

or

malmostshar@yahoo.com

If you wish to receive the file in Word format, please send us an email message and we will send it to you immediately.

After completing the application, you will receive the full analysis and a report containing the memories of your subconscious mind, and the secrets behind the motives of your behaviour.

For any enquiries, please contact us through these email addresses:

info@ihossa.com

or

malmostshar@yahoo.com

Dr MAHMOUD